W9-BRT-707

PARENTS
Like Mine

Marie-Therese Miller

Special thanks to Stephanie Garrity, Executive Director of Rainbows for All Children

Lerner Publications ◆ Minneapolis

To my parents, Lylian and Harold, with gratitude and love

Lerner Publications Company
An imprint of Lerner Publishing Group, Inc.
241 First Avenue North
Minneapolis, MN 55401 USA

For reading levels and more information, look up this title at www.lernerbooks.com.

Main body text set in Mikado a.
Typeface provided by HVD Fonts.

Editor: Allison Juda **Designer:** Emily Harris

Library of Congress Cataloging-in-Publication Data

Names: Miller, Marie-Therese, author.
Title: Parents like mine / Marie-Therese Miller.
Description: Minneapolis : Lerner Publications, [2021] | Series: Many ways | Includes bibliographical references and index. | Audience: Ages 5–9. | Summary: "Parents can be mom and dad, dad and dad, single parents, stepparents, and more. Explore the many ways that diverse parents care for children"– Provided by publisher.
Identifiers: LCCN 2019049871 (print) | LCCN 2019049872 (ebook) | ISBN 9781541598058 (library binding) | ISBN 9781728413716 (paperback) | ISBN 9781728400167 (ebook)
Subjects: LCSH: Parents–Juvenile literature. | Families–Juvenile literature.
Classification: LCC HQ755.8 .M5525 2021 (print) | LCC HQ755.8 (ebook) | DDC 306.874–dc23

LC record available at https://lccn.loc.gov/2019049871
LC ebook record available at https://lccn.loc.gov/2019049872

Manufactured in the United States of America
1-47996-48674-2/10/2020

OurFamilyWizard is proud to offer the Many Ways series. Since 2001, OurFamilyWizard has been dedicated to supporting communication between parents who are raising kids from separate homes. Over the years, the understanding of what a family looks like has changed. But no matter a family's shape or size, the meaning of family has always remained rooted in love and respect. We hope these books help children learn the many different ways to be.

Table of Contents

All Kinds of Parents

PARENTS love and take care of you. You are special to them.

You **LEARN** and **LAUGH** together.

Kids can have a mom and a dad.

They might **COOK** and eat together.

Some kids have two moms or two dads.

They could all **PLAY** at the park.

Kids can have one mom or one dad.

They might make **FUNNY FACES** and giggle together.

Relatives, such as grandmas and grandpas, can take care of children.

Their family might **CUDDLE** and read stories.

Some **PARENTS** are married. Other **PARENTS** are not married.

Either way, they help their kids **FEEL BETTER** when they are sick.

Parents might share the same HOME.
Parents might live apart.

Wherever they live, parents can **HELP** their kids with homework.

Some parents have to travel for work.
Military moms or dads can be **DEPLOYED**.

These families can send drawings and letters to keep in touch.

Some parents **GIVE BIRTH** to their kids.

Other parents **ADOPT** or **FOSTER** their children. Stepparents raise children too.

Whatever kind of parents you have, they want you to be happy. **THEY LOVE YOU.**

Glossary

adopt: to make a child a part of your family forever

apart: not together

deployed: sent somewhere for military service

foster: to parent a child without adopting the child

homework: schoolwork that is done at home

military: having to do with soldiers or the armed forces

relative: a family member

together: with one another

Further Reading

Cavell-Clarke, Steffi. *Different Families.* New York: Crabtree, 2018.

Families Change: Kids Guide to Separation and Divorce
https://www.familieschange.ca.gov/en/kids

Kerley, Barbara. *Brave like Me.* Washington, DC: National Geographic, 2016.

Miller, Marie-Therese. *Families Like Mine.* Minneapolis: Lerner
Publications, 2021.

Swinton, Patty. *What's Life like with a Single Parent?* New York:
PowerKids, 2019.

"You, Me & Community: Come and See—PBS KIDS"
https://www.youtube.com/watch?v=YsfMWr3nyEM&feature=youtu.be

Index

Photo Acknowledgments

Image credits: stevecoleimages/E+/Getty Images, p. 4; MoMo Productions/DigitalVision/Getty Images, p. 5; shapecharge/E+/Getty Images, p. 6; JGI/Tom Grill/Getty Images, p. 7; FG Trade/E+/Getty Images, p. 8; monkeybusinessimages/iStock/Getty Images, pp. 9, 16, 20; MNStudio/iStock/Getty Images, p. 10; Carina König/EyeEm/agency/Getty Images, p. 11; LaylaBird/E+/Getty Images, p. 12; Alistair Berg/DigitalVision/Getty Images, p. 13; fizkes/iStock/Getty Images, p. 14; Tetra Images/Brand X Pictures/Getty Images, p. 15; Hero Images/Getty Images, p. 17; U.S. Army National Guard photo by Sgt. 1st Class Dexter Miller, p. 18; Morsa Images/DigitalVision/Getty Images, p. 19; DNF Style/Shutterstock.com, p. 21; Shaw Photography Co./Moment/Getty Images, p. 22.

Cover: michaeljung/iStock/Getty Images (top left); kate_sept2004/E+/Getty Images (top right); LeoPatrizi/E+/Getty Images (bottom left); monkeybusinessimages/iStock/Getty Images (bottom right).